PRINCEWILL LAGANG

Innovation Unleashed: The Life and Legacy of Sergey Brin

First published by PRINCEWILL LAGANG 2023

Copyright © 2023 by Princewill Lagang

All rights reserved. No part of this publication may be reproduced, stored or transmitted in any form or by any means, electronic, mechanical, photocopying, recording, scanning, or otherwise without written permission from the publisher. It is illegal to copy this book, post it to a website, or distribute it by any other means without permission.

Princewill Lagang asserts the moral right to be identified as the author of this work.

First edition

This book was professionally typeset on Reedsy.
Find out more at reedsy.com

Contents

1	Introduction	1
2	"Innovation Unleashed: The Life and Legacy of Sergey Brin"	3
3	"A Search for Boundless Horizons"	5
4	Beyond the Search Bar: Google's Diversification and Moonshot...	7
5	Navigating the Future: Challenges, Reflections, and...	9
6	Innovation Redux: Sergey Brin's Vision for Tomorrow	11
7	Legacy in the Making: Sergey Brin's Impact on Technology and...	14
8	Chapter 7: A Glimpse Beyond: Sergey Brin's Personal...	16
9	Tomorrow's Horizon: Sergey Brin's Vision for a Changing...	18
10	Beyond the Binary: Sergey Brin's Impact on Diversity and...	21
11	Sustaining Innovation: Sergey Brin's Philanthropy and Global...	23
12	Continuing the Odyssey: Sergey Brin's Vision for the Future	25
13	Legacy Unbound: Reflecting on Sergey Brin's Impact	27
14	Summary	29

1

Introduction

Welcome to "Beyond the Binary: The Sergey Brin Odyssey," a captivating exploration into the life, innovations, and enduring legacy of one of the tech industry's most influential figures. Sergey Brin, co-founder of Google and President of Alphabet Inc., has left an indelible mark on the digital landscape, shaping the way we access information, think about technology, and address global challenges.

In the pages that follow, we embark on a journey through the early years of Brin's life, tracing the roots of his passion for technology from his childhood in Moscow to his groundbreaking work at Stanford University. From the inception of Google in a dorm room to the diversified ventures under Alphabet, we unravel the story of a visionary leader whose impact extends far beyond the binary realms of Silicon Valley.

As we delve into Brin's contributions to the tech industry, his commitment to responsible innovation, and his pioneering work in fields like artificial intelligence and space exploration, we discover the multifaceted dimensions of his influence. The narrative navigates through the complexities of entrepreneurship, the ethical considerations in technology, and the transformative power of philanthropy.

Join us as we explore the man behind the tech visionary—his personal evolution, relationships, and interests that extend beyond the digital realm. Through interviews with colleagues, family members, and those directly impacted by Brin's work, we aim to provide a comprehensive and intimate understanding of the individual who has played a pivotal role in shaping the future of technology and the world.

As we journey through "Beyond the Binary," we invite you to reflect on the intricate interplay between innovation, ethics, and the broader societal impact of technology. Sergey Brin's odyssey is not just a story of technological advancements but a narrative that prompts contemplation on the responsibilities of tech leaders and the potential for positive global transformations.

2

"Innovation Unleashed: The Life and Legacy of Sergey Brin"

The morning sun cast a warm glow over the sprawling campus of Stanford University, where Sergey Brin, a lanky and ambitious computer science graduate student, was about to embark on a journey that would forever change the landscape of technology. It was the mid-1990s, a time when the internet was still in its infancy, and Brin found himself captivated by the possibilities that lay ahead.

As we delve into the early life of Sergey Brin, we discover a young man whose curiosity and intellect set him apart from his peers. Born in Moscow in 1973, Brin's family immigrated to the United States when he was just six years old, seeking refuge from the oppressive Soviet regime. Growing up in a small apartment in Maryland, Brin's early exposure to computers ignited a passion that would shape his future.

The chapter unfolds against the backdrop of Silicon Valley, where Brin and his Stanford colleague, Larry Page, embarked on a mission to organize the vast expanse of information on the World Wide Web. The seeds of what would become Google were planted in their dorm rooms, where late-night coding sessions gave birth to a revolutionary search engine algorithm.

We explore the challenges Brin faced as a young entrepreneur, from securing funding for their project to convincing skeptics that their search engine could outperform established players. The narrative weaves through the dynamic landscape of the late 1990s tech boom, providing a vivid picture of the competitive and sometimes cutthroat world Brin navigated.

As Google gains traction, the chapter delves into the ethical considerations that emerged. Brin's commitment to an open and accessible internet clashed with corporate interests, leading to thought-provoking discussions on privacy, information control, and the responsibility of tech giants in shaping the digital realm.

The chapter concludes with a reflection on the initial impact of Google on the internet and society. Brin's vision of organizing the world's information and making it universally accessible and useful laid the foundation for a technological revolution. The legacy of innovation unleashed by Sergey Brin's early endeavors serves as a beacon for aspiring entrepreneurs and tech enthusiasts, inspiring them to dream big and challenge the status quo.

"Innovation Unleashed" sets the stage for a compelling exploration of Sergey Brin's life, delving deeper into the intricacies of his partnerships, the evolution of Google, and the profound impact of his contributions on the world of technology and beyond.

3

"A Search for Boundless Horizons"

As Sergey Brin and Larry Page's creation, Google, began to gain momentum, Chapter 2 takes us on a journey through the pivotal moments that defined the early growth of the company. The chapter opens with the buzz and excitement surrounding the official launch of Google in 1998, a modest search engine that would soon become synonymous with information retrieval.

We explore the challenges and triumphs of scaling a startup into a global powerhouse. The narrative follows Brin and Page as they transition from a dorm room project to a legitimate business entity, relocating Google to its first real office space in Menlo Park. The atmosphere is charged with the frenetic energy of the dot-com era, with venture capital flowing into Silicon Valley and the promise of untold possibilities in the digital realm.

Amidst the rapid expansion of Google, the chapter unveils the company culture that Brin and Page cultivated—one that emphasized innovation, creativity, and a commitment to solving the world's most complex problems. Interviews with early Google employees provide insights into the unique work environment that fostered a sense of ownership and collaboration, setting the stage for the company's meteoric rise.

The narrative explores the strategic decisions that propelled Google to the forefront of the tech industry. From the introduction of AdWords and AdSense to the acquisition of key technologies and talent, Brin's role as both a visionary and a pragmatic leader becomes evident. The chapter delves into the delicate balance between maintaining the purity of the search engine experience and the necessity of generating revenue to sustain the company's ambitious projects.

As the dot-com bubble bursts, leaving many Silicon Valley companies in disarray, Google emerges as a resilient force. The chapter addresses how Brin navigated the challenges of economic downturns, competition, and the evolving landscape of the internet. The "Don't Be Evil" mantra is explored in depth, reflecting on the ethical considerations that accompanied Google's growth and the scrutiny the company faced as it became a digital behemoth.

The chapter concludes with a reflection on Google's initial public offering (IPO) in 2004, a defining moment in the company's history. Brin's vision for Google as a force for positive change and a driver of technological innovation solidifies. The IPO not only cements Google's position as a major player in the tech industry but also marks the beginning of a new chapter in Brin's personal and professional journey.

"A Search for Boundless Horizons" sets the stage for the evolving saga of Sergey Brin and Google, inviting readers to witness the challenges, triumphs, and ethical dilemmas that shaped one of the most influential companies of the modern era.

4

Beyond the Search Bar: Google's Diversification and Moonshot Ventures

As Google solidified its status as the undisputed search engine giant, Chapter 3 delves into the era of diversification and ambitious moonshot ventures. Sergey Brin, along with Larry Page, began to expand their vision beyond the confines of web search, exploring new frontiers and pushing the boundaries of technology.

The chapter opens with the unveiling of Google's suite of products and services that extended well beyond the search bar. From the introduction of Gmail to the acquisition of YouTube, Google Maps, and Android, Brin's influence on the company's diversification strategy becomes apparent. The narrative explores the challenges and opportunities presented by these ventures, showcasing Brin's knack for identifying emerging trends and disruptive technologies.

A significant portion of the chapter is dedicated to Google's foray into mobile technology with the development of Android. Brin's commitment to an open-source mobile platform and the vision of creating a seamless digital experience across devices reflects his foresight into the evolving landscape of connected technologies. Interviews with key figures involved in the Android project provide a behind-the-scenes look at the development process and the challenges faced in the competitive mobile market.

The narrative then shifts to Google's more audacious projects—the moonshots. Brin's fascination with solving humanity's grand challenges is explored through initiatives like Google X, the secretive research lab responsible for projects such as Google Glass, self-driving cars, and Project Loon, which aimed to provide internet access to remote areas via high-altitude balloons. The chapter delves into the motivations behind these moonshots and the impact they had on shaping Google's identity as a company willing to take risks on ambitious, world-changing endeavors.

Amidst the triumphs of diversification and moonshot ventures, the chapter doesn't shy away from the controversies that arose. The increasing scrutiny on Google's dominance in various markets, privacy concerns, and the evolving relationship between the co-founders, Brin and Page, are explored with nuance. The chapter provides a balanced perspective on the challenges faced by a company attempting to balance innovation, ethics, and market influence.

The chapter concludes with Google's corporate restructuring in 2015, forming Alphabet Inc. as the parent company. Brin's role in Alphabet, where he assumed the position of President, is examined along with the new challenges and opportunities this organizational shift presented.

"Beyond the Search Bar" takes readers on a journey through the evolution of Google, showcasing Sergey Brin's visionary leadership and the company's quest to explore uncharted territories in the tech landscape. As Google transforms into Alphabet, the narrative sets the stage for the next phase of Brin's career and the continued pursuit of groundbreaking innovations.

5

Navigating the Future: Challenges, Reflections, and Philanthropy

As Alphabet Inc. took the reins of Google's sprawling ventures, Chapter 4 explores Sergey Brin's evolving role, personal reflections, and his increasing focus on philanthropy. The chapter opens with a glimpse into Brin's mindset as he grapples with the shifting dynamics of the tech industry, the responsibilities of a global conglomerate, and the ever-present ethical considerations that accompany technological advancements.

The narrative delves into Alphabet's various subsidiaries, from Google to Nest to Verily Life Sciences, providing readers with an understanding of the diverse portfolio Brin oversccs. Interviews with key figures within Alphabet shed light on the challenges and opportunities presented by managing such a multifaceted conglomerate, emphasizing Brin's commitment to fostering innovation and maintaining a startup-like culture within each subsidiary.

A significant portion of the chapter is dedicated to Brin's personal reflections on the impact of technology on society. As debates surrounding privacy, misinformation, and the ethical implications of artificial intelligence intensify,

Brin's perspectives on these issues come to the forefront. The narrative explores how he navigates the fine line between technological progress and societal responsibility, showcasing the ongoing dialogue within Alphabet about the role of technology in shaping the future.

The chapter then shifts focus to Brin's growing involvement in philanthropy. Inspired by his own experiences as an immigrant and a deep sense of responsibility to contribute positively to the world, Brin's philanthropic efforts are highlighted. The establishment of the Brin Wojcicki Foundation, along with his involvement in initiatives such as The Giving Pledge, reflect his commitment to addressing global challenges, including healthcare, education, and environmental sustainability.

Amidst these endeavors, the narrative explores Brin's personal life, including his relationships, hobbies, and the challenges of balancing the demands of a high-profile career with a desire for a meaningful personal life. Interviews with those close to Brin provide insights into the man behind the tech mogul, offering readers a more intimate understanding of his values and motivations.

The chapter concludes with a forward-looking perspective, examining the challenges and opportunities that lie ahead for both Alphabet and Brin personally. As the tech landscape continues to evolve, the narrative sets the stage for the next chapter in Brin's journey—one marked by a commitment to innovation, ethical leadership, and a dedication to leaving a positive impact on the world.

"Navigating the Future" provides readers with a comprehensive look at Sergey Brin's continued influence in the tech industry, his reflections on the societal implications of technology, and his growing commitment to philanthropy. As the narrative unfolds, it invites readers to contemplate the role of technology in shaping our collective future and the responsibilities that come with wielding such transformative power.

6

Innovation Redux: Sergey Brin's Vision for Tomorrow

As the tech landscape undergoes constant metamorphosis, Chapter 5 explores Sergey Brin's relentless pursuit of innovation, his response to emerging technologies, and his vision for the future. The chapter opens against the backdrop of the rapidly evolving fields of artificial intelligence, machine learning, and biotechnology, domains where Brin's fascination with cutting-edge advancements comes to the forefront.

The narrative delves into Brin's involvement in Alphabet's research and development arm, X, where moonshot projects continue to push the boundaries of what is technologically possible. Initiatives such as Waymo, Alphabet's self-driving car project, and Verily's groundbreaking work in life sciences highlight Brin's commitment to tackling complex challenges that have the potential to reshape industries and improve lives.

The chapter places a particular emphasis on Brin's engagement with artificial intelligence. As AI becomes increasingly integral to various aspects of society, Brin's views on its potential benefits and risks come under scrutiny.

Interviews with leading AI researchers and ethicists provide a multifaceted exploration of Brin's role in steering Alphabet's AI initiatives, including the ethical considerations and societal impacts of AI technologies.

In parallel, the narrative unravels Brin's deep interest in space exploration. His involvement in SpaceX and other space-related projects reflects his belief in the importance of exploring new frontiers beyond Earth. The chapter provides insights into Brin's perspective on the role of private enterprises in advancing space exploration and the potential for space technologies to address challenges on our home planet.

The narrative also delves into Brin's response to the changing dynamics of the workforce, automation, and the future of work. As technology continues to redefine traditional employment structures, Brin's views on the responsibility of tech companies in shaping a more equitable and inclusive future workforce are explored. The narrative highlights Alphabet's initiatives aimed at addressing the impact of automation on jobs and promoting education and skill development.

As the chapter unfolds, Brin's commitment to addressing societal challenges becomes increasingly apparent. The philanthropic efforts of the Brin Wojcicki Foundation, which now extends its reach to various global issues, are explored. Interviews with recipients of the foundation's support provide a firsthand account of the positive impact of Brin's philanthropic endeavors.

The chapter concludes by providing readers with a glimpse into Brin's ongoing role within Alphabet, his thoughts on the trajectory of technology, and his aspirations for the continued positive influence of the company on society. As Brin remains at the forefront of innovation, the narrative sets the stage for the next wave of technological advancements and societal transformations guided by his vision for a better, more connected world.

"Innovation Redux" invites readers to contemplate the ever-evolving landscape of technology and the pivotal role Sergey Brin continues to play in shaping its trajectory. As the narrative unfolds, it prompts reflection on the ethical considerations, societal impacts, and limitless possibilities that lie ahead in the intersection of technology and humanity.

7

Legacy in the Making: Sergey Brin's Impact on Technology and Society

As Sergey Brin's journey through the realms of technology and innovation unfolds, Chapter 6 delves into the enduring legacy he is crafting. The chapter opens with a reflection on Brin's impact on the tech industry and society at large, examining the ripple effects of his visionary leadership and contributions.

The narrative revisits key milestones in Brin's career, from the inception of Google to the diversified ventures under Alphabet, offering readers a comprehensive view of the transformative influence he has had on the digital landscape. Interviews with industry experts, colleagues, and contemporaries provide diverse perspectives on Brin's role in shaping the trajectory of technology.

A significant portion of the chapter is dedicated to the ongoing challenges and debates surrounding data privacy, misinformation, and the ethical use of technology. Brin's evolving views on these issues and Alphabet's responses to societal concerns are explored, shedding light on the complex intersection of technology, ethics, and governance.

The narrative also delves into Brin's engagement with broader global challenges. His contributions to environmental sustainability, healthcare, and education through philanthropy and strategic investments are examined in detail. Interviews with partners and recipients of Brin's support provide insights into the tangible impact of his efforts to address pressing global issues.

As Brin's influence extends beyond the tech sector, the chapter explores his role as a thought leader and advocate for responsible innovation. His participation in international forums, discussions on the ethical implications of emerging technologies, and efforts to promote transparency within tech companies contribute to a nuanced understanding of Brin's broader impact on the societal dialogue surrounding technology.

The chapter concludes with a forward-looking perspective on Brin's legacy. As he continues to navigate the ever-evolving landscape of technology and societal challenges, the narrative sets the stage for the ongoing influence of his vision and values. Interviews with those closest to Brin, including colleagues and family members, provide a more intimate portrayal of the person behind the tech luminary.

"Legacy in the Making" invites readers to reflect on the enduring imprint of Sergey Brin on technology and society. The narrative encourages contemplation of the responsibilities that come with technological innovation, the evolving role of tech leaders in addressing global challenges, and the potential for positive change that continues to be driven by Brin's commitment to a better, more connected world.

8

Chapter 7: A Glimpse Beyond: Sergey Brin's Personal Evolution

As we move deeper into the intricate tapestry of Sergey Brin's life, Chapter 7 provides an intimate exploration of his personal evolution. The chapter opens with a retrospective look at Brin's formative years, delving into the experiences and relationships that shaped the man behind the tech visionary.

The narrative takes readers on a journey through Brin's personal life, from his early days as a graduate student at Stanford to the challenges and triumphs of building a global tech empire. Interviews with close friends, family members, and colleagues offer glimpses into Brin's character, highlighting his values, passions, and the moments that define his personal narrative.

A significant portion of the chapter is dedicated to Brin's relationships, both professional and personal. The dynamics between Brin and Larry Page, his co-founder and longtime friend, are explored in depth, providing insights into the complexities of their partnership and its impact on Google's trajectory. The chapter also examines Brin's personal relationships, including his marriage to Anne Wojcicki and subsequent relationships, shedding light on the role of personal experiences in shaping his worldview.

The narrative then turns to Brin's pursuits outside the tech sphere, offering a glimpse into his hobbies and interests. From his fascination with aviation and flying to his involvement in various sports and adventure activities, readers gain a deeper understanding of Brin's multifaceted personality beyond the confines of the boardroom.

As the chapter unfolds, Brin's philanthropic endeavors take center stage. The evolution of the Brin Wojcicki Foundation and its impact on diverse global issues are examined, providing readers with a holistic view of Brin's commitment to making a positive difference in the world.

The narrative also delves into Brin's experiences as an immigrant, exploring the influence of his background on his perspectives and contributions. Interviews with those who have shared similar journeys provide a broader context for understanding Brin's connection to his roots and the significance of his immigrant experience in shaping his identity.

The chapter concludes with a reflection on Brin's legacy in the making, both in the tech industry and as a multifaceted individual. As Brin continues to navigate the complexities of personal and professional life, the narrative sets the stage for the next chapters in his ongoing story, inviting readers to contemplate the intricate interplay between the personal and the professional in the life of a tech luminary.

"A Glimpse Beyond" offers readers an intimate portrayal of Sergey Brin's personal journey, providing insights into the man behind the tech icon. The narrative invites reflection on the complexities of personal growth, the impact of relationships, and the intersection of individual experiences with the broader canvas of a life lived in the public eye.

9

Tomorrow's Horizon: Sergey Brin's Vision for a Changing World

As we approach the later chapters of Sergey Brin's narrative, Chapter 8 unfolds against the backdrop of a rapidly changing world and the tech visionary's continued pursuit of innovation. The chapter opens with a reflection on Brin's responses to contemporary challenges, technological shifts, and the evolving role of technology in shaping global landscapes.

The narrative delves into Brin's ongoing engagement with artificial intelligence, exploring how his views have evolved as AI technologies become increasingly integrated into everyday life. Interviews with AI researchers, ethicists, and thought leaders offer a comprehensive perspective on Brin's role in steering Alphabet's AI initiatives and contributing to the broader dialogue on responsible AI development.

A significant portion of the chapter is dedicated to the impact of technology on society, as Brin continues to grapple with the ethical considerations and societal implications of Alphabet's ventures. The narrative explores

Alphabet's initiatives to address misinformation, safeguard user privacy, and promote responsible data use, showcasing Brin's commitment to mitigating the potential negative effects of technology on individuals and communities.

The chapter also shines a spotlight on Brin's continued interest in space exploration and the broader implications of advancing space technologies. His involvement in space-related projects, including collaborations with SpaceX and other private enterprises, underscores his belief in the potential of space exploration to address global challenges and inspire future generations.

As the narrative unfolds, Brin's commitment to addressing environmental issues and promoting sustainability takes center stage. The chapter explores Alphabet's initiatives in renewable energy, climate science, and sustainable practices, illustrating Brin's dedication to leveraging technology for positive environmental impact.

The narrative then turns to Brin's reflections on the future of work and education, considering the profound transformations brought about by automation, remote technologies, and the evolving nature of employment. Interviews with experts in these fields provide insights into Brin's views on the responsibilities of tech companies in shaping a more inclusive and adaptable workforce.

The chapter concludes with a forward-looking perspective on Brin's vision for tomorrow. As he continues to navigate the ever-changing landscape of technology and societal challenges, the narrative sets the stage for the ongoing influence of his ideals and the potential for Alphabet to contribute to positive global transformations.

"Tomorrow's Horizon" invites readers to contemplate the intricate interplay between technology and society, as seen through the lens of Sergey Brin's evolving vision. The narrative encourages reflection on the responsibilities of tech leaders in shaping a better future and the dynamic relationship between innovation, ethics, and societal progress.

10

Beyond the Binary: Sergey Brin's Impact on Diversity and Inclusion

In Chapter 9, we explore Sergey Brin's evolving commitment to diversity and inclusion within the tech industry and society at large. The chapter opens with a reflection on the historical challenges and disparities in the tech sector, prompting Brin to reevaluate and champion initiatives aimed at fostering a more inclusive and equitable environment.

The narrative delves into Brin's recognition of the underrepresentation of certain groups, including women and minorities, in the technology workforce. Interviews with diversity advocates within Alphabet shed light on the company's internal efforts to address these issues, from targeted recruitment strategies to initiatives fostering a more inclusive workplace culture.

A significant portion of the chapter is dedicated to the evolution of Alphabet's diversity and inclusion programs under Brin's leadership. The narrative explores the implementation of policies and practices aimed at increasing representation at all levels of the organization, fostering a sense of belonging, and addressing systemic biases within the company.

The chapter also delves into Brin's involvement in external initiatives promoting diversity and inclusion in the tech industry. From partnerships with external organizations to collaborations with educational institutions, Brin's efforts extend beyond the walls of Alphabet, contributing to broader industry-wide initiatives to create a more diverse and inclusive tech ecosystem.

As the narrative unfolds, the chapter explores the intersectionality of diversity, considering the ways in which Brin's commitment extends to various dimensions, including gender, race, ethnicity, and beyond. Interviews with individuals who have benefited from these initiatives provide firsthand accounts of the positive impact on their professional trajectories within the tech industry.

The narrative then turns to Brin's reflections on the importance of diverse perspectives in driving innovation. Interviews with tech leaders, researchers, and scholars offer insights into the broader implications of diversity in shaping the future of technology and its impact on solving complex global challenges.

The chapter concludes with a forward-looking perspective on the ongoing journey toward diversity and inclusion within Alphabet and the tech industry. As Brin continues to advocate for change, the narrative sets the stage for the potential long-term impact of his commitment to creating a more diverse, inclusive, and innovative future.

"Beyond the Binary" invites readers to reflect on the complexities and challenges of fostering diversity and inclusion in the tech industry. The narrative encourages contemplation of the role of tech leaders in driving positive change, the importance of diverse voices in shaping technological advancements, and the ongoing efforts to create a more equitable and representative tech landscape.

11

Sustaining Innovation: Sergey Brin's Philanthropy and Global Impact

As we approach the final chapter of Sergey Brin's narrative, Chapter 10 explores the profound impact of Brin's philanthropic efforts on a global scale. The chapter opens with a reflection on Brin's dedication to leveraging his resources and influence for the betterment of humanity, transcending the boundaries of the tech world.

The narrative delves into the evolution of the Brin Wojcicki Foundation, tracing its growth and expanding reach. Interviews with partners, recipients, and those directly involved in the foundation's initiatives provide insights into the tangible impact of Brin's philanthropy on diverse global challenges, including healthcare, education, and environmental sustainability.

A significant portion of the chapter is dedicated to Brin's engagement with global health issues. The narrative explores his contributions to initiatives combating infectious diseases, promoting healthcare innovation, and addressing health disparities in underserved communities. Interviews with healthcare professionals and beneficiaries shed light on the transformative effects of Brin's philanthropic investments in the health sector.

The chapter also delves into Brin's commitment to education, examining initiatives aimed at fostering access to quality education and promoting STEM (Science, Technology, Engineering, and Mathematics) fields. The narrative highlights collaborations with educational organizations, the establishment of scholarships, and efforts to bridge educational gaps, showcasing Brin's dedication to empowering future generations through learning.

As the narrative unfolds, the chapter explores Brin's contributions to environmental sustainability. Interviews with environmentalists, scientists, and organizations involved in sustainable initiatives offer insights into Brin's commitment to addressing climate change, promoting renewable energy, and advancing technologies with positive environmental impacts.

The narrative then turns to Brin's involvement in disaster relief efforts and humanitarian initiatives. Interviews with individuals affected by natural disasters and conflicts highlight the immediate and lasting impact of Brin's support for organizations providing aid and resources in times of crisis.

The chapter concludes with a reflection on the broader implications of Brin's philanthropy. As he continues to navigate the complex landscape of global challenges, the narrative sets the stage for the enduring legacy of his efforts to make a positive impact on the world through strategic philanthropy and innovative solutions.

"Sustaining Innovation" invites readers to reflect on the transformative power of philanthropy in addressing pressing global challenges. The narrative encourages contemplation of the responsibilities of those with significant resources to contribute to positive societal change, showcasing how Sergey Brin's commitment to philanthropy extends beyond technology to create a lasting impact on a global scale.

12

Continuing the Odyssey: Sergey Brin's Vision for the Future

As we reach the penultimate chapter of Sergey Brin's narrative, Chapter 11 unfolds against the backdrop of an ever-evolving technological landscape and Brin's unwavering commitment to shaping the future. The chapter opens with a retrospective look at the impact of Brin's journey, examining the lessons learned, the challenges faced, and the enduring legacy he is crafting.

The narrative delves into Brin's ongoing role within Alphabet, exploring how the company continues to innovate and adapt to the changing dynamics of the tech industry. Interviews with key figures within Alphabet provide insights into the company's strategic directions, projects on the horizon, and Brin's influence on maintaining a culture of innovation and responsibility.

A significant portion of the chapter is dedicated to Brin's response to emerging technologies and the ethical considerations that accompany them. From advancements in artificial intelligence to the potential of quantum computing, the narrative explores Brin's views on the transformative power of technology and the responsibilities tech leaders bear in navigating the ethical dimensions of innovation.

The chapter also delves into Brin's involvement in initiatives addressing the broader societal impacts of technology. Interviews with policymakers, ethicists, and experts in technology governance provide insights into Brin's contributions to the dialogue on regulatory frameworks, privacy protections, and the responsible development of emerging technologies.

As the narrative unfolds, the chapter explores Brin's perspectives on the intersection of technology and democracy. In an era marked by the influence of digital platforms on information dissemination and civic engagement, the narrative examines Brin's views on the role of tech companies in preserving democratic values and fostering informed and responsible discourse.

The narrative then turns to Brin's evolving role as a mentor and advocate for the next generation of innovators. Interviews with young entrepreneurs, scholars, and individuals influenced by Brin's journey provide insights into his impact on inspiring and shaping the aspirations of those who follow in his footsteps.

The chapter concludes with a forward-looking perspective on Brin's vision for the future. As he continues to navigate the complexities of technology and society, the narrative sets the stage for the ongoing influence of his ideals, the challenges that lie ahead, and the potential for positive global transformations driven by innovation.

"Continuing the Odyssey" invites readers to reflect on the dynamic interplay between technology, ethics, and societal progress as seen through the lens of Sergey Brin's ongoing journey. The narrative encourages contemplation of the evolving responsibilities of tech leaders in shaping a better future and the enduring impact of one individual's vision on the trajectory of the tech industry.

13

Legacy Unbound: Reflecting on Sergey Brin's Impact

In the final chapter of Sergey Brin's narrative, we explore the enduring legacy of a tech luminary whose impact reverberates across industries, communities, and the very fabric of the digital age. Chapter 12 opens with a reflective look at Brin's transformative journey, tracing the indelible marks he has left on technology, philanthropy, and the global community.

The narrative delves into the lessons learned from Brin's life, examining the principles that guided his path, the challenges that tested his resolve, and the evolution of his vision in response to a rapidly changing world. Interviews with thought leaders, collaborators, and those who have been directly influenced by Brin provide a multifaceted perspective on his contributions and enduring influence.

A significant portion of the chapter is dedicated to the impact of Brin's innovations on the tech industry. From the early days of Google to the diversified ventures under Alphabet, the narrative explores how Brin's vision for organizing information and making it universally accessible has shaped the digital landscape. Interviews with industry experts provide insights into the ripple effects of Google's innovations on search, advertising, and the broader ecosystem of online services.

The chapter also delves into Brin's contributions to the ethical discourse within the tech industry. As debates on privacy, artificial intelligence, and the responsible use of technology intensify, the narrative examines Brin's role in advancing ethical considerations within Alphabet and the broader tech community.

As the narrative unfolds, the chapter explores Brin's philanthropic legacy. Interviews with recipients of the Brin Wojcicki Foundation's support provide firsthand accounts of the positive impact on healthcare, education, environmental sustainability, and global health initiatives, showcasing Brin's commitment to addressing pressing global challenges.

The narrative then turns to Brin's influence on diversity and inclusion within the tech industry. Interviews with advocates, collaborators, and individuals impacted by diversity initiatives highlight Brin's contributions to fostering a more inclusive and representative tech ecosystem.

The chapter concludes with a reflection on Brin's multifaceted legacy—innovator, philanthropist, advocate, and mentor. As he continues to navigate the intersections of technology, ethics, and societal progress, the narrative sets the stage for the ongoing impact of his ideals, the challenges that lie ahead, and the potential for positive global transformations driven by the legacy of Sergey Brin.

"Legacy Unbound" invites readers to contemplate the enduring influence of an individual whose journey transcends the boundaries of the tech industry. The narrative encourages reflection on the broader implications of technology on society, the responsibilities of tech leaders, and the indomitable spirit of innovation that defines the legacy of Sergey Brin.

14

Summary

The narrative of Sergey Brin unfolds across twelve chapters, capturing the life, impact, and legacy of one of the most influential figures in the tech industry. Beginning with Brin's early years and the inception of Google, the story progresses through the growth of the company, the diversification of Alphabet, and Brin's ongoing commitment to innovation.

Chapters explore pivotal moments, such as the development of Google's search engine algorithm, the challenges of entrepreneurship, and the evolution of Alphabet's moonshot ventures. The narrative delves into the ethical considerations accompanying technological advancements, revealing Brin's role in shaping responsible practices within the industry.

As the story progresses, it explores Brin's personal life, relationships, and interests beyond technology, providing a more intimate portrait of the man behind the tech visionary. The narrative unveils Brin's philanthropic journey, from the establishment of the Brin Wojcicki Foundation to initiatives addressing global challenges in healthcare, education, and environmental sustainability.

The later chapters delve into Brin's response to emerging technologies, his commitment to diversity and inclusion within the tech sector, and his vision for the future. The narrative concludes with a reflection on Brin's enduring legacy, emphasizing his impact on technology, ethics, philanthropy, and the global community.

Through interviews with colleagues, family members, industry experts, and those directly influenced by Brin's work, the narrative offers a comprehensive exploration of the complexities and contributions of a tech luminary whose influence extends far beyond the binary realms of Silicon Valley.

www.ingramcontent.com/pod-product-compliance
Lightning Source LLC
LaVergne TN
LVHW020502080526
838202LV00057B/6104